HOPE ISLAND

An Adventure of Self-Discovery
and Personal Growth

DONNA BARDELL

Workbook and References Included

Copyright © 2019 Donna Bardell.

ALL RIGHTS RESERVED. This book contains material protected under International and Federal Copyright Laws and Treaties. Any unauthorized reprint or use of this material is prohibited. No part of this book may be reproduced or transmitted in any form or by any means, electronic or mechanical, including photocopying, recording, or by any information storage and retrieval system without express written permission from the author/publisher.

Paperback: 978-1-64184-175-7
Ebook: 978-1-64184-176-4

To my parents for your three-plus decades of sobriety.
To my siblings for your strength and courage.
To my children for your compassionate hearts.
You are my inspiration.

ACKNOWLEDGEMENTS

The love, support and encouragement of family and friends was the fuel that fed this book. I am humbled by those who read early versions of the story and provided insightful feedback. Louise Peters, Mandy Bass, Susan Arslanian, Carolyn Hendricks, Tomi Helm, M.J. Rennaker, Saska Richards, Tonya Kelly, Mary Salakie, Peggy Zorn, and Mani Powers, it gives me great joy to read the parts of the book that reflect your suggestions. A piece of you lives within the story. I cherish that.

Linda Villegas Bremer, your Spanish translation enabled this resource to have a significantly larger reach. Thank you for donating your time and talent.

Dr. Becky Bailey, the years I worked with you and taught Conscious Discipline® were transformative for me. Your seven Powers and seven Skills gave me a healthy framework for living. They are so much a part of me that they are inevitably reflected within the book.

I especially want to thank my parents, Don and Judy, and my siblings, Brian, Lance, Tracy and Darren.

The beauty of our family's story of healing and recovery is one of the things I am most proud of in my life. I honor the work each of you have done in your journey toward wholeness. Over the years, we have individually and collectively suffered tragedy, yet have converted loss into love. We have taken responsibility for our actions, forgiven trespasses, and maintained compassionate hearts. I celebrate your strength and courage, and I love you completely.

Lastly, I want to thank my children, Evan and Ashley. You two had no choice but to travel with me on my journey toward wholeness. Through every stage you have shown me unwavering, unconditional love, regardless of how difficult things were for you. I see your powerful lights. Shine them upon the world!

Disclaimer

While the characters in this story are fictional, their experiences are common. Any resemblance to actual persons is coincidental. The activities in the workbook are designed to support one's healing process but are not a substitute for professional counseling and care.

CONTENTS

PROLOGUE ix
CHAPTER 1   BIRTHDAY. 1
CHAPTER 2   MOLDAVITE. .11
CHAPTER 3   BROKEN. 15
CHAPTER 4   FREEDOM. 21
CHAPTER 5   GRACE 29
CHAPTER 6   TRUTH 37
CHAPTER 7   HOPE. 43
WORKBOOK 45
HELP 73

PROLOGUE

The wind blew hard against Sophia's face as she paddled frantically across the water, forcing the stream of tears to roll across her cheeks and drip into her ears. She wasn't going to stop to dry them. Her wrinkled forehead and stern expression were only slight indicators of the rage she felt. The waves chopped around the kayak, now the only thing she had left from her grandma. The morning had started so bright and sunny; now the sky was slate gray. The clouds moved rapidly overhead as if they were late for an appointment. Sophia sensed the rain was coming, but all she could focus on was escaping to her safe place on Hope Island.

It had been three years since Sophia's grandmother had died, and she had been escaping to the nearby island ever since. It was only a few hundred yards from her home, yet today it felt like a day's journey to get there. The seagulls chased her the entire paddle out, swooping overhead and screeching at her with what sounded like, "Hurry! Get out of here! Hide!" Although it was exhausting, Sophia didn't stop paddling until she made it to the island. She first heard the bottom of the kayak scratching against the rocks, sand, and shells before she realized she had made it to the shore. She dragged the vessel up the beach and into the woods, safe from the tide washing it away, stealing her only way back home. The dark clouds began to release a light rain, setting it free to cleanse the earth. Sophia ran down a path deep into the island, panting as adrenaline continued to surge through her veins. She knew the island's thick trees would protect her from the weather.

When Sophia found her favorite hiding spot, she unbuckled the three snaps of her life jacket and laid it on the ground. She curled up into a ball under the dark tree canopy, resting her head on the foamy device. She allowed herself to begin to feel the grief that she had been numb to all these years. She began to sob. It was slow at first, like a faucet left partially on, and then built like an orchestra's crescendo into an explosion rooted deep in her gut. The release ended in a scream at the top of her lungs. In this wooded sanctuary she cried for the insanity of her home life. She cried for her early loss of innocence. She cried for her grandma. She cried for the emptiness she felt at the core of her being. Sophia was startled by the guttural sounds that came from within her, yet she allowed the teary faucet to run on full.

CHAPTER 1
BIRTHDAY

It was Sophia's tenth birthday, and she and Grandma Judy prepared for a special camping trip to Hope Island. Grandma Judy was an avid hiker and camper and knew how to pack for this overnight adventure. She had travelled all over the world visiting different countries and cultures with only a backpack. She put that expertise to use as she showed Sophia how to store the camping supplies in the two backpacks they were taking with them to the island. Once their packs were set, they strapped them on and began their walk to the community marina where Grandma Judy's kayak was stored.

As they walked to the marina, Sophia thought about how special her neighborhood was. Her house was surrounded by trees and overlooked the inlet. She could see a mountain range from her front porch. She could also watch deer cross her yard as they fed upon the plants in her garden. Sophia couldn't remember a single day when she didn't see a deer. They were always around.

When they spotted her, they would freeze in place with a stare, waiting to decide who should move first – the human or the deer. It would be three years before Sophia would understand her special connection with deer.

After walking just a few minutes, they arrived at the marina. Sophia and her grandma took the tandem kayak off the storage rack and carried it to the water only a few feet away. Sophia felt like a racehorse at the gate, ready to run. She got in the front kayak seat. Grandma Judy launched them from the shore and hopped in the backseat. As soon as they began to paddle in the direction of Hope Island, two brown speckled seals surfaced above the water, swimming playfully alongside the kayak. It was as if they were in on the birthday celebration. The spirited mammals would dive into the cool water and periodically pop their whiskered noses out, gazing with their dark chocolate eyes directly into Sophia's. Seals always made her smile. Their gentle demeanor reminded her of her Labrador Retriever. They seemed so innocent, especially the seal pups. Some days Sophia would walk out to the end of the pier and watch the seals sun themselves on the logs tied to the pylons. The pylons were designed to break the wake of the tugboats and motorboats that would travel past the community marina. The seals seemed to think the logs were custom-designed lounge chairs for them.

The sun was beginning to set when Grandma Judy and Sophia arrived at the island for the birthday celebration. They carried the kayak onto shore and placed their belongings on the ground. It was time for their shared ritual of watching the sun retire over the distant mountains. On this special day, the sky was a watercolor canvas with pinks, blues, purples, oranges, and gold.

Grandma Judy said, "Let's do our Salute to the Sun!"

Together, Sophia and the family matriarch stood facing the descending globe. As her grandma had taught her, Sophia took a deep breath in through her nostrils, imagining she was inhaling love through her heart. On the exhale she focused on her appreciation of the surrounding beauty. Her chest gently moved up and down. Her body relaxed.

The two began in unison, "I raise my hands to the radiant sun," as they stretched their arms up toward the setting sun. They then opened their arms wide in a V-shape saying, "I welcome its light shining on us as one." Next, they chanted, "I wave to the eagle flying high in the sky," as they swayed their arms back and forth. Then, bringing their arms to their sides, they rolled their shoulders several times as they said, "I shrug off my worries to let them flow by." This was followed by, "I touch the land surrounded by sea," as they reached to feel the grass next to their feet. To finish, they stood facing each other, looking directly into each other's eyes. While creating heart shapes with their fingers, they closed with, "I see love's light in you and me."

Sophia gave her grandma a big grin. It was in these moments that Sophia felt happiest. Grandma Judy looked deeply into Sophia's eyes. She put her hands upon her granddaughter's shoulders and pulled the child close to her body. Sophia could hear her grandma's heartbeat as she rested her right ear against her grandma's chest. Sophia remained in her embrace for a full minute, their breathing in sync. Sophia turned to take in the brilliant palette of colors in the sky as the sun's light danced off the puffy clouds over the hills and mountains. She fully appreciated what "purple mountain majesty" meant in *America the Beautiful*.

"We'd better set up camp before it gets dark," Grandma Judy said.

Sophia slipped her arms through the straps of her backpack and swung it into place on her back. She helped her grandma put her pack on; it contained the sleeping bag and tent, and then the two of them followed the path around the island.

Excursions to Hope Island with Grandma Judy were always a special occasion, but tonight was extra special. Her grandma had told her the entrance into "double-digit living" was a rite of passage. She said that the number ten was very powerful. The number one represented a new beginning and zero amplified the power of the number one. She told Sophia this day was the start of a new life for her. Sophia wasn't sure what it all meant, but she liked the way it sounded.

As they walked through the trail, Sophia noticed imprints in the clay dirt path from other hikers who had been there and noticed the rust-colored bark peeling off the Madrone trees. Every few steps she'd see highlights from the last bit of sun peeking through the branches. She loved this Pacific Northwest island and the way it made her feel so close to nature. Suddenly, a squirrel raced across the path in front of Sophia and scurried up an evergreen tree. As Sophia's eyes followed the squirrel, she noticed how thick and tall the tree was and wondered about its age. She was curious over the number of years the tree had stood watch over the island while making a home for animals and a hideaway for humans. She thought, "When I'm grown up, I'm going to build a home among the trees overlooking the water."

"Grandma Judy, what's your favorite thing about Hope Island?" asked Sophia, as they hiked the trail around the island perimeter.

"Oh, my goodness, it's impossible for me to pick one thing about the island since there is so much beauty living here," her grandma replied. "I can pick the one thing it makes me feel … connected!"

Sophia gave her grandma a puzzled look. "Connected to what?" she asked.

"Connected to all that is … connected to myself."

"What do you mean, Grandma Judy? How are you connected to everything and connected to yourself?"

Grandma Judy stopped walking, turned to look at her grandchild and said, "We've got a beautiful view of the mountain from here. Let's set up camp and I'll explain over dinner."

They set down their backpacks and quickly canvassed the area to find wood pieces to build a campfire. Grandma Judy picked up some larger rocks to create a boundary to contain the fire. She carved out a fire pit in the clay using one of the rocks with a sharp edge. Sophia stacked the wood as her grandma had taught her to do when she was little. With a pocket lighter, Grandma Judy lit the dry needles and twigs she had placed underneath the wood. Within minutes they had a warm, soothing fire crackling under the evening sky.

Next, the birthday girl and her beloved grandma unpacked their backpacks. They set up their small tent, unraveled the sleeping bags, and placed them inside the tent along with their other belongings. Grandma Judy laid a blanket on the ground not far from the campfire. Sophia got the water out of her backpack and filled each of their cups. She set them on the blanket next to the plate of sandwiches her grandma had packed, along with a bag of frozen grapes. Sophia noted how perfect their simple meal was. She picked her spot on the blanket and sat down. Grandma Judy sat next to her. They looked out over the water, watching the last remnants of the dazzling sunset.

Once the sun disappeared behind the mountains, Grandma Judy stated it was time for a gratitude reflection. Staying seated and cross-legged, they turned to face each other and held hands. Grandma Judy said, "Divine Creator, everywhere present in all beings and things. We are grateful for the plants and animals that gave of themselves to nourish our bodies. We are thankful for the kayak and paddles that made it possible for us to travel to this place of beauty. We appreciate the opportunity to join in celebration of Sophia's ten years of life on this sacred planet. We open our hearts and receive this love with gratitude."

Sophia always loved her grandma's gratitude reflections. They had the power to still her, creating a calm within she only experienced when she was with her grandma.

"Let's eat!" Grandma Judy exclaimed.

As they enjoyed their food, Sophia noted to herself how far away her house on the mainland felt even though she could physically see lights shining through the windows of her neighbors' homes.

"Grandma …" Sophia began.

"Yes, Precious?"

"… What did you mean by feeling most connected to all that is and to yourself when you come here?"

The sixty-five-year-old woman looked at Sophia and said, "May I ask you a question first?"

Sophia nodded.

"What's *your* favorite thing about this island?" Grandma Judy inquired.

Sophia laughed. "I love so many things about this place! I love the tall trees and the trails beneath. I love the way the plants pop with color in the spring. I love how quiet it is. I love all the different birds and animals that make it home. I love the mountain views and vibrant sun rises and sunsets. Most of all, I love that I forget about everything else in my life."

Grandma Judy smiled lovingly at her grandchild, and in a warm voice said, "You have perfectly described what 'being connected to all that is and to myself' means. The spark of life force that created the plants and animals on this island and everything on the planet is the same spark within you and me. Whenever I'm in nature, especially here on Hope Island, I am reminded of this truth. We are connected to everyone and everything. That's why it's so important to honor and respect other people and the planet. When we harm another, we are harming ourselves, and vice versa."

Sophia wrinkled her brow as she always did when she was in deep thought. She considered her grandma's words and they felt right. She also felt a heavy sadness.

"Grandma ... why does dad drink and behave the way he does? And why does mom pretend everything is fine? I hate it! Don't they know about this connection?"

Grandma Judy pulled her grandchild close to her side, hip to hip, and put her left arm around the child.

"Sophia, when people are hurtful they are acting out their own pain. Most people don't realize the connection we are talking about. Think of it as sleepwalking through life, unconscious of our connection to everything and unaware of our impact. Just as you are becoming aware, it is possible for your mom and dad to wake up from the dream – or nightmare – they are in and start anew."

Sophia quickly replied, "But haven't you tried to wake them up?"

Grandma Judy looked at her grandchild and said, "Of course I have, my beloved. They're not ready to awaken, but I have hope they will."

"Hope! That's the name of the island we're on!" Sophia said, delighted.

The two sat silent for a few minutes, their eyes following sparks from the campfire floating upward amid the faint smoke. They gazed at the stars that were just beginning to sparkle through the silent indigo sky. Suddenly they heard a deep howl off in the distance. Sophia looked at her grandma with wide eyes.

"You're safe, my child. That call is coming from another island," Grandma Judy said with a smile while resting a comforting hand on the girl's thigh. "You know, it's a gift to hear the wolf use its voice to express itself. And speaking of gifts, it's time for your present!"

This surprised Sophia; she thought the camping trip was her birthday gift. She watched Grandma Judy unclasp the silver necklace from around her neck that carried a raw piece of forest green moldavite. She had worn it for as long as Sophia could remember. Grandma Judy got to her knees and maneuvered behind Sophia, clasping the revered jewelry around her granddaughter's neck.

"Grandma Judy!" exclaimed Sophia. "You're giving this to me … to keep?"

"It is now time for you to be the keeper of this gemstone. For decades it has reminded me of my connection to all that is. I want you to wear this as a reminder of Creation's spark within you."

Sophia was honored to wear her grandma's necklace. She had always admired the irregularly shaped gem. Never had she imagined that she would one day wear it.

Grandma Judy noticed Sophia's joyful expression. She placed her hands on the sides of her granddaughter's face and gently kissed each cheek. She pulled back, looking directly into the girl's eyes. With a tender voice she whispered, "Happy Birthday, Sophia. I love you, and the Source that created all that is loves you. Always remember there is nothing you can do or experience that can alter that spark within you. You are love and you are surrounded by love always. You are never, ever alone."

Sophia couldn't contain her joy. She threw her arms around her grandma, causing the two of them to fall backward onto the blanket with a playful giggle. They rolled onto their backs and looked up at the shimmering stars. Sophia felt the warmth of the fire and the warmth of her grandma's love. With her mind she took a snapshot of the joyful moment, storing it in her heart. She would need it later.

CHAPTER 2
MOLDAVITE

In the morning, the bright orange sun shone through the evergreen trees and between the cracks of the flap covering the entrance to the tent. Sophia sat up and noticed that her grandma was not next to her. Her body shivered from the chill of the damp air and the loss of warmth from her grandmother's body. She reached to her chest to feel the moldavite necklace and smiled to herself. Sophia felt lucky. She couldn't imagine having had a more special birthday celebration. Grandma Judy always made life better.

The ten-year-old quickly put on her sweat jacket and hiking shoes before stepping out of the tent to find her beloved camping companion. She noticed the outside of their shelter was now covered with moist droplets, as was the grass, dirt, leaves, and every other surface she could see. The smell of the burned wood from their evening campfire lingered. As Sophia inhaled the scent, she felt the cool morning air move through her nostrils.

She looked up and saw Grandma Judy sitting at a picnic table facing the ever-present mountain across the water.

"Good morning grandma!" Sophia shouted.

"Well, good morning," Grandma Judy replied, "What a fabulous sunrise this morning! The sky was neon pink as the sun came up behind the mountain. How I do love a good sunrise."

"And a good sunset!" exclaimed Sophia.

Grandma Judy looked at Sophia with the heartfelt smile the girl trusted so well. She patted a spot on the towel-covered bench next to her, signaling Sophia to come sit by her side. When she got to the picnic table, Grandma Judy stood with open arms. Sophia nestled herself into her grandma's chest, soaking up the loving embrace she relied upon.

After allowing her grandma's love in, the two sat side-by-side looking out over the water at the sunlit mountain. Sophia reflected on the conversation she had last night with her grandma. She loved how she could talk to her about anything; she also loved how she could simply sit with Grandma Judy and say nothing. After a few minutes Grandma Judy broke the silence.

"Are you hungry? I can get the granola bars and apples from the bag in the bear box."

"Yes, please grandma," she replied. Grandma Judy walked over to the metal box provided at their campsite to keep their food safe from hungry or curious animals. She unlatched the box and gathered the food and drink supplies. She then carried the breakfast items to the picnic table where Sophia remained, and set up the continental-style breakfast.

After they finished eating, they packed up their campsite. Sophia poured water over the remaining campfire embers, and the two began their hike back to the kayak. When they arrived at the tandem craft, they picked it up and carried it to the same spot where they landed on the beach the day before. Again, Sophia seated herself upfront.

As they started to paddle back to the mainland, the ten-year old turned her head to look back at her grandma, eyeing Hope Island in the background.

"Grandma Judy … thank you for making my tenth birthday so special. It was the best birthday ever! I'm never going to take off your moldavite necklace."

"Now it's *your* moldavite necklace," the grandmother emphasized. "I'm glad you are happy, honey. I am too! You light up my world."

When they arrived at Sophia's house it was nearly ten o'clock in the morning. Grandma Judy walked Sophia inside. Her mom was up but her dad was still in bed. "Hi, mom! We're back," Sophia exclaimed.

"How was your camping trip?" her mom asked as she washed dishes. She didn't stop what she was doing or even turn to look at Sophia.

Sophia glanced at her grandma, who was gazing back at her with an understanding look. "It was great! Grandma Judy gave me her moldavite necklace!"

"She gave you her what?" questioned Sophia's mom.

"Her moldavite necklace! It's that glassy green gemstone she always wears on a silver chain. Grandma Judy told me moldavite is a projectile rock formed by a meteorite impact nearly 15 million years ago…and now it's mine!"

"How nice," her mother replied, still washing dishes and staring out the window over the sink.

Sophia looked down at the floor and said, "I'm going to head up to my room." She walked over to her grandma with noticeably less energy than when she entered the house and gave her a long hug. She whispered, "I love you," in her grandma's ear. The older woman replied with the same, then Sophia turned and went upstairs. She had no way of knowing that would be the last time she would hug Grandma Judy or hear her voice.

CHAPTER 3
BROKEN

Even though it had been three years since Sophia's grandmother had died, the depth of loss made it feel like yesterday. She had learned to live without the loving embrace of Grandma Judy and found that using her imagination to speak to her helped ease the grief. Some days Sophia would paddle out to Hope Island and sit on the pebbled shore when the tide was out. She would close her eyes and recall the snapshot in her mind of her tenth birthday. She easily recollected the image of the two of them lying under the stars after her grandma explained to her about the spark within that connects her to all that is. It was the same night she gave Sophia her moldavite necklace. Sophia's memories of her grandma, combined with the still, cool water and air, were a sure remedy for the upset Sophia often felt. Being in nature with Grandma Judy used to make the tandem kayak paddle out to Hope Island a soothing ritual of renewal for Sophia. Now when she made the short traverse to her safe place, she did it solo and she did it to escape her home life.

Sophia's other place to escape was her best friend Tara's home. The girls met when they entered middle school and hit it off right away. Tara had become like a sister. They would finish each other's sentences and sometimes didn't even need to speak to know what the other was thinking. They could look at each other and simply nod with understanding. Sophia shared everything with Tara. All her family secrets were locked in the safe of Tara's mind. Sophia was thankful to have someone she could talk to and not worry about being judged or criticized.

In her own home she continued to feel alone. One time she asked her mom why she didn't tell someone about her dad's drinking. Her mom's response was, "It's none of anyone's business what goes on in this home. We don't air our dirty laundry in public!" Sophia felt ashamed of the things her dad did to her at night and concluded from her mother's declaration that *she* was the dirty laundry.

With Grandma Judy gone, Tara made life bearable. Tara's parents were divorced and her mom went out most nights. There was nothing Sophia could say about her family that Tara wouldn't understand. For Sophia, Tara was her virtual safe place. The two girls talked each night before bed, which helped Sophia put her bedtime fears aside and go to sleep. Sophia didn't know what she would do if she didn't have her friend.

Last evening, Sophia arrived at Tara's house after dinner. Tara's mom was going to be out late, and Tara was responsible for watching her little brother. After she put him to bed, Tara and Sophia sat on the back porch listening to their favorite electronic dance music. The weather was perfect. A slight breeze periodically brushed their faces, drawing their attention to the beauty of the night.

In that moment Sophia felt safe. It was a relief not to have to worry about drunken visits from her father.

"Tara ... do you know where your mom goes at night when she leaves you here to watch your brother?"

"I'm not sure. There's a bar and restaurant in town I know she likes to go to. A couple of years ago they called the house asking for someone to come and get her because she had fallen off a bar stool onto the floor. I told them there was no one here who could do that. I didn't know how she was going to get home and was worried about her all night. When I finally fell asleep, she still wasn't home. I woke up in the middle of the night because I heard some noises coming from the living room. I decided to go see if it was my mom, but when I got halfway down the stairs I could see her lying on the living room floor making out with some guy I've never seen before. Their clothes were off ... I was mortified!"

Sophia put her hand on her friend's shoulder, looked her in the eyes, and asked, "What did you do?"

"I turned and ran upstairs! I jumped in bed and put the covers over my head. I was crying and my body was shaking. I felt sick."

"Did your mom know you saw her?"

"Yes! She came up to my room right away and sat next to me on my bed. She pulled the covers away from my head and asked me what was wrong. I looked right at her and told her I saw her naked on the floor with some stranger. She told me I was having a dream ... that it wasn't real ... but I know what I saw! There she was, sitting next to me with nothing on and trying to convince me that my eyes had been playing tricks on me. She made me question myself; that has really stuck with me."

Sophia pulled Tara close to her and gave her a gentle hug.

"I'm so sorry, Tara. That sucks."

Sophia's tenderness triggered tears from Tara. They slowly followed the contours of the girl's face down to her chin and onto Sophia's shoulder.

The two girls sat quiet for several moments until Sophia broke the silence: "I know what it's like to feel like you're going crazy."

The girls separated from their embrace and locked eyes.

"Ever since I was a little girl taking naps, my dad has been coming into my room while I sleep. I used to wake up from a nap and there he was, naked in bed with me. It made me feel so gross inside. The earliest memory I have in my life is when I was around three years old. I woke up from what I call my "Chase Dreams," where I am running down a dark, wet alley, trying to get away from someone who is running after me. I never see who it is; I don't turn and look back, I just run! I have Chase Dreams just about every night; I wake up exhausted every morning."

This time it was Tara who did the consoling. She picked up Sophia's right hand and clasped it between both of hers. She didn't interrupt her friend. Her simple gesture communicated love and support.

Sophia continued, "For the past 10 years my dad has been coming into my room while I'm sleeping. When I was little I didn't know any better, but now I do, and it disgusts me."

Sophia started to sob.

"I feel damaged … broken! How can anyone ever love me?"

Tara reached for a tissue and gave it to her friend. Sophia blew her nose, then continued.

"What drives me crazy is we never talk about it; we pretend it isn't happening, as if it's all just a dream, similar to what your mom wanted you to believe about her and that guy."

Tara nodded her head, and then asked, "Does your mom know?"

"I assume she does. I don't see how she couldn't be aware of him coming into my room; it's a small house and it's been going on for as long as I can remember."

"Now I know why you like spending the night at my house," Tara said.

"Yep!" was Sophia's simple response.

Even though talking about Sophia's dad was upsetting for her, she also felt a little lighter after sharing more of her secret with Tara. Unfortunately, that reprieve was short-lived.

When Sophia arrived home from Tara's house the next morning, her father was throwing a fit. He stood over her mother, who was seated at the kitchen table with a plate of bacon, eggs and toast in front of her. His face was so close to hers that he was spitting in her ear as he unveiled his wrath upon her.

"You can't do anything right! How hard is it to put bacon on a frying pan and cook it? You don't pay attention to what you're doing!"

Something inside of Sophia snapped. She had had enough of his bullying. She dropped her overnight bag at the front door and ran over to her parents.

"Stop it!" she yelled at her dad, "You can't talk to mom that way!"

When Sophia was a foot away from her father, she planted her feet firmly on the kitchen floor and stared fiercely into his raging eyes.

"Why can't you just leave us alone?"

Her boldness surprised her. It surprised her parents as well. Without blinking, her father slapped Sophia across her right cheek, sending her flying to the laminate floor. He then stood over her, bent down, grabbed the moldavite necklace, and yanked it off Sophia's neck. She felt a burning sensation in the back of her neck where the necklace had been, but it was no match for the fire in her belly as she watched her father throw the moldavite necklace against the refrigerator door, shattering the glass gemstone into several pieces. Sophia couldn't believe her eyes. In an instant her connection to her grandmother and the strength she channeled from her were gone.

"I hate you! You ruin everything good!" Sophia cried.

She swiftly got up and went to the front door, grabbed her backpack, and ran out of the house, slamming the door behind her. Next she seized her bicycle and life jacket from the carport and rode down to the marina where her grandmother's kayak was stored. She needed to escape from the maddening home life in which she felt trapped.

In less than two minutes Sophia was in the parking area next to the kayak racks. She dropped her bicycle on the gravel lot. With a tear-stained face, she dragged the kayak to the water, got in, and paddled with a fury out to Hope Island. Not once did she turn to look at the life she wanted to leave behind.

CHAPTER 4
FREEDOM

Sophia's heart and body were spent. She used every ounce of energy she had to paddle to the island. The weight of her grief compounded her fatigue. When she made it to her favorite spot – her tenth birthday campsite – she sat down under the trees, which protected her from the light rain. Her eyes were set across the water to the distant mountain. She thought about that camping trip and how it was the last paddle out to Hope Island with Grandma Judy before she suddenly passed away. Sophia had felt so safe with her grandmother; now she felt completely lost.

As she laid on the ground, her head resting on her life jacket, she recalled the howl of the wolf she and Grandma Judy heard on that birthday night; she wondered if it had been calling for help. Right now, Sophia wanted to howl. She began to cry; her sobs audible to any creature nearby. Eventually she let out a guttural scream. The ongoing flow of tears blurred her vision;

her eyelids were getting heavy. The water and mountain were now fuzzy; so was her head.

Sophia heard the crack of a stick and sat up. She blinked her eyes several times to try to focus. She looked behind her and was surprised to see a majestic wolf sitting in the center of the trail, gazing back at her. He had bright amber eyes, which sharply contrasted the white, black, and gray fur in his face and body. Sophia sensed this wolf would not harm her, so she got off the ground and slowly walked over to him.

When Sophia was next to the animal, she squatted down and held her palm open for the wolf to smell.

"Hi, fella," she said, "who are you?"

Sophia heard a response from the wolf, but it was not with her ears. It was as if the wolf spoke deep within her.

"My name is Freedom," said the wolf. "I am your guide for the journey ahead. Will you follow me? There is something I want you to see."

Sophia smiled in agreement. The wolf turned and began to lead her through the forest. She followed the muscular animal down a narrow path between an array of humungous trees. All she could see was plant life all around her and a ceiling of evergreen branches overhead. The ground was hard, and occasionally Sophia had to step over a thick root that traversed the trail. There was complete silence except for the birds chirping from the tree canopy. Every so often Freedom would turn his head and give Sophia a reassuring look. She felt connected to this wolf in an inexplicable way.

After several minutes of hiking into the forest, Sophia heard a faint trickling sound in the distance. Freedom took a right turn off the path, making his own trail toward the sound. He led the girl to a cool stream. She noticed a change in temperature and a fresh quality to the air as she stood by the water's edge. The curious girl knelt on the grassy edge to feel the water with her hands; she couldn't believe how pure and clear it was. She smiled as she gazed at the collage of multi-colored pebbles covering the stream floor and tiny bright fish riding the current over them.

The girl and the powerful animal sat together at the edge of the stream. Without thinking, Sophia put her hand on Freedom's back and began to stroke his fur. She noticed how much thicker and rougher his coat was than her dog's. She also noticed how natural it felt to be with him; it was as if he had always been a part of her life.

After a few minutes of enjoying the peaceful scene, Freedom broke the silence: "Sophia, I have been watching over you for the past thirteen years. I've seen the courage with which you face your difficult family circumstances. I have also seen how tightly you bundle up your feelings inside, especially anger. Tell me what happened for you this morning when you walked into your home and saw your parents in the kitchen."

Sophia's eyes teared up as she told Freedom how she found her father yelling at her mother over burned bacon and how she lunged in to rescue her.

"I couldn't take his bullying another minute! He doesn't care about anyone but himself! He treats my mom and I like we're objects at his disposal to do with what he wants. It's like we don't matter; we're not important. I couldn't take it any longer."

Freedom lifted his head up, and with his golden eyes looked directly at the tear-stained girl.

"How did that feel, Sophia, to use your voice with your dad?"

The girl paused for a moment, her eyes raising in the direction of the tree canopy, as if recalling images in her mind. She then looked back at Freedom and replied, "I felt strong at first … until he hit me."

The wolf leaned into Sophia. He bent his head down, resting the top of his forehead in the middle of her chest. Sophia scratched Freedom behind his ears. He took a deep breath in, and as he exhaled Sophia felt a warmth inside of her own heart.

Freedom then looked up at her and said, "It was a courageous thing for you to do, standing up for your mom. You were also standing up for yourself. Do you see that, Sophia?"

The girl looked Freedom in the eyes and nodded her head.

"Setting boundaries with others is very important. That's what you were trying to do with your dad. Unfortunately, your dad is not in a place in his life where he is able to listen, and it became unsafe. Your safety is of the utmost importance, Sophia. There are adults outside of your home who will listen to you and help you. Can you think of an adult you trust that you can speak to?"

Sophia thought about her favorite teacher, Miss Shekinah. She always smiled at Sophia when she greeted her at the start of class. She also spent extra time with her after school helping with homework. Often Miss Shekinah would tell her, "There is a bright future in store for you, Sophia. Don't give up." Sophia wanted to believe what Miss Shekinah said was true. She considered the possibility of telling her teacher the same secrets she had shared with Tara.

Suddenly Sophia had several different emotions come to the surface at once. She felt angry with her father for how he treated her and her mom. She felt angry with her mom for not protecting them. She felt sorrow over her broken moldavite necklace. She felt relief at the possibility that she didn't have to keep things a secret anymore and that there might be help. Sophia noticed the tightness that had been in her throat slowly relax.

She looked into Freedom's amber eyes and confessed, "I feel safe with Miss Shekinah, my math teacher, but I feel nervous about telling on my dad."

Freedom nodded his head with understanding. "Sophia, I know it can be scary speaking about these things, especially to someone outside of your family. Miss Shekinah is a good choice. She may need to get some other helpers involved with protecting you. You have a right to be safe and you need help to do that."

With a crack in her voice, Sophia replied, "... I want it to stop."

"Sophia, talking to a trusted adult about what is going on at home is an important thing to do for your safety. It will also help move energy that can get stuck in your body when you feel scared or upset. Emotions are intended to arise, inform you of how you are feeling, and then be released. Talking to someone about how you are feeling helps to do that."

The attentive girl flashed back in her mind to how she felt lighter the night before after telling Tara about her dad's visits to her room.

"Think of it this way: the 'E' in the word 'emotion' stands for energy and the rest of the word is 'motion.' Your feelings are like this stream; the continuous movement maintains the clarity. If you hold your fear and anger inside of you, it can create an internal dam, blocking their flow. That block can disconnect you from your instincts and intuition. As you allow yourself to feel your emotions and then release them, you keep that energy moving. This will help you stay connected to your True Self, who you really are.

Sophia listened intently to Freedom. She wanted the heaviness in her heart to leave her.

The wolf continued.

"In addition to talking to someone about what is happening in your life, can you think of some physical things you enjoy doing that will also help this energy to flow?"

The 13-year old thought for a moment and replied, "I love music and dancing. Sometimes I put my earbuds in, play my favorite tunes on my phone with the volume on high, and dance around my bedroom."

"Brilliant! Dancing is a great way to connect with your body and move energy. Practicing your grandmother's 'Salute to the Sun' stretches in front of the mirror could work, too."

Sophia's eyes lit up. She had forgotten about the ritual she and Grandma Judy would do every time they arrived on Hope Island. She nodded enthusiastically.

Freedom paused for a moment. Then, with a serious look in his eyes he softly said, "Allowing your feelings to flow like this stream can set you free. To symbolize this, bend down, cup your hands together and take a drink from it. Imagine the water flushing your harbored hurt feelings away."

Sophia followed Freedom's guidance. She knelt at the edge of the stream, cupping her hands together. She filled them with the crisp, clean stream water and took a drink. The water felt light and fresh as Sophia swallowed it. She closed her eyes and pictured the anger she felt toward her dad and mom as a raging campfire. She envisioned the fresh water putting the fire out, with nothing but smoke remaining. She opened her eyes. The fire in her belly was gone.

Freedom noticed Sophia's shoulders drop and her face relax. There were no longer signs of anguish in her body. Sophia smiled at her wolf guide and wrapped her arms around his thick, furry neck. She hugged him tight and put her face in his coarse fur coat. As she held him close, she inhaled his musky scent, which made her smile. She decided in that moment that the next time she felt scared or angry she would think of her musky friend, put on her ear buds and dance. She may even buy a musk-scented candle to light in honor of Freedom!

"I believe you're ready to meet Grace," Freedom told her.

Sophia looked curiously at him and asked, "Who is Grace?"

"You'll find out shortly," he replied. "She, too, cares for you deeply."

CHAPTER 5
GRACE

    Sophia followed Freedom as they walked farther into the forest. She kept one hand on the wolf's wooly back and the other outstretched to touch the plants and trees along the path. She loved the earthy smell and textures of the forest. For the first time, Sophia felt the heaviness she always lived with begin to lift from her chest.
    When they were deep among the trees, Sophia noticed a family of whitetail deer off in the distance. She stopped in her tracks to focus on the family, as their natural camouflage made them nearly invisible. They reminded her of the deer she came across at home. It always delighted her the way they stood still when they noticed she was present, staring her in the eyes as if to tell her something, and then gracefully leaping off in the opposite direction.
    "Oh! I think I know who Grace is!" Sophia exclaimed.

Freedom looked up at her, his eyes twinkling. He led her in the direction of the deer family still gazing at them. There were two spotted fawn, a buck with felt-covered antlers beginning to sprout, and a large doe. As Sophia and Freedom got closer, the fawns took off into the forest with the buck following close behind. The doe remained, awaiting Sophia's arrival.

"Hello, Grace!" Sophia cheerfully said.

"Hello, Sophia," came a quiet response from within the thirteen-year old girl, "it's good to finally meet you. I've been waiting for this day for a long time."

"You know who I am … and you've been waiting for me? How can that be?"

The deer walked closer to Sophia, stopping when they were face-to-face. Grace's tender ebony eyes drew Sophia in, creating a powerful connection between them.

"I have been keeping an eye on you since you were a little girl. Will you walk with me?" Sophia glanced at Freedom, who gave her an approving look, and replied, "Sure!"

Grace and Sophia leisurely followed the wooded trail. Freedom gave them space but was not far behind. The girl noticed the abundance of vibrant green foliage outlining the path. It stood out against the russet and gray bark on the trees scattered throughout the forest. Grace stopped next to a giant Douglas-fir tree. Sophia knew the type of evergreen it was by its thick, deeply furrowed bark. When she was little, Grandma Judy taught her about the different trees in the region; this one was easily recognizable by its outer layer.

"Sophia, tell me what you see when you look at this tree," Grace requested.

Sophia reached out with her right hand and felt the exterior of the tree. She ran her palm along the rough surface, allowing her fingertips to explore the grooves of the bark.

"I see chunky bark on the outside ..." she announced, while looking closely at the tree.

Sophia continued to move her hand across the bark while her eyes scanned the tree. When she looked down, she spotted a snail at the base of the tree. Its shell was reddish-brown with a dark band running along the periphery.

"Look at the snail, Grace! Its colors are beautiful!"

Sophia crouched down to get a closer look and Grace moved in next to her.

"Yes, it is," agreed Grace. "What do the snail and the tree have in common, Sophia?"

The girl looked at the tiny creature clinging to the bark, and it occurred to her that each was encased.

"Well, they both have outer layers that protect them. The Douglas-fir has a thick bark and the snail has a hard shell."

"That's a very good observation, Sophia," the deer responded. "I see some similarities with you as well."

The girl turned to look at Grace, confused.

"You are as regal as this tree and have the gentleness of this snail. Although you weren't born with a hard, protective outer layer, you have created an invisible shield around your heart to guard it. While it's natural to want to build a barrier to keep pain out, that same barrier keeps love from getting in."

Sophia thought about the idea of a shield. The image of her mother came to mind. She could see how her mom's shield made her numb. Some days her mom seemed like an empty shell. Sophia didn't want to become lifeless like that.

As if Grace heard the girl's thoughts, she said, "You can put your shield down, Sophia. Creation's spark is always within you. It can empower you to heal and grow from any situation and begin again. Just as the buck's antlers are discarded each winter, they grow back in the spring regardless of the kind of winter it has been for the buck. You have the same resilience and power to regenerate after any painful life event. You are not defined by your parents' actions or by what has been done to you. By being still you can connect to your own power, to the spark within you."

This didn't make sense to Sophia. She couldn't imagine how being still could give her power.

"I don't understand, Grace. How does that work? After my dad hit me and broke my moldavite necklace, I ran out of my house and paddled to Hope Island. There was no way I could be still. I didn't want to be in that house another minute. All I could think about was getting as far away as I could!"

The doe gazed into the girl's eyes with a gentleness that conveyed deep understanding.

"Sophia, being safe is critical. Your instincts told you to flee. As Freedom shared with you earlier, your instincts contain insight that is vital. Just as you've seen my kind standing still as statues and in the next instant leaping away into the forest for safety, your instincts tell you when to do the same."

Sophia listened intently to the doe.

"In the situation you experienced at home this morning with your dad, physical movement was necessary to keep you safe. I imagine your emotions were high at that time. May I ask what you were feeling when you took off from your house and paddled out to Hope Island?"

Sophia gave Grace an empty look as if she didn't know.

"When you are unsure of how you are feeling, becoming still can help you access your inner wisdom," the animal advised. "If you'd like, we can practice stilling your mind and body so you know how to do it."

Sophia told Grace she wanted to learn. She sat down on the forest floor, crossed her legs, and eagerly awaited the deer's coaching.

Grace guided Sophia to take three deep breaths. She told her on each inhale to say to herself, "Peace to my mind," and on the exhale, "Still my thoughts and body."

Sophia followed her instructions.

After the girl took her third breath, Grace whispered to her, "Now relax, breathing normally. Focus on your breathing the way your Grandma Judy taught you."

After a minute of silence Grace instructed, "If you notice your thoughts wandering, simply repeat, 'Peace to my mind. Still my thoughts and body.' Continue to breathe naturally."

Sophia sat silent for several minutes, practicing stilling herself. Suddenly the words, "How could he do this? ... It's not my fault ... I feel all alone," popped into her head. She didn't know where the words came from, but she knew they were hers.

"Grace! I got a message!" Sophia exclaimed.

The deer laid down on the ground next to Sophia, her legs folded beneath her. The doe's proximity to the girl was a comfort. Grace looked directly at Sophia.

"You connected to your wise one within. Do you have more insight into what you've been feeling?" Grace asked softly.

Sophia quickly responded, "I feel like I'm on my own to take care of myself. It's like my parents put me in a kayak without a paddle and pushed me into the ocean inlet. They are supposed to take care of me, not send me out to sea! I feel so angry with them! I thought if I behaved and didn't upset my dad, then he wouldn't get drunk and hurt my mom and me. For years I've felt ashamed; I didn't want anyone to know what was going on in my home. My best friend, Tara, is the only person I've told. Now, after stilling myself, I realize none of this is my fault!"

Grace looked lovingly at the girl and responded, "It makes perfect sense you would feel abandoned and angry."

The doe then rested her head on Sophia's lap. Sophia stroked Grace's soft tawny fur coat. Tears began to stream down her cheeks. Freedom and Grace sat in silence, honoring the child's grief.

After releasing some of her heartache, Sophia used her jacket sleeve to wipe the tears off her face. She then looked at Grace.

The deer sensed some of Sophia's grief had lifted and asked, "How are you doing?"

Sophia gave the deer a slight smile and replied, "Better."

Grace then advised her that she always has access to her heart, her wise one within.

"Try to make time to be still each day to connect with your heart – maybe first thing in the morning or at night before you go to bed."

Sophia said she would. With that, the girl and the deer arose and moved to where Freedom was patiently waiting.

"You can do this, Sophia. Believe in yourself," Freedom said confidently.

Grace gave Sophia the same look of assurance and said, "It's time for me to rejoin my family and time for you to meet one more friend today."

The girl thanked Grace for teaching her how to still herself so she could connect with her wise one within. She tightly embraced the doe, her arms wrapped completely around her neck.

After the hug, Sophia said good-bye to Grace. The endearing deer leaped off in the same direction as her family had gone.

Sophia looked at Freedom and asked, "Where to next?"

Freedom looked at her with what appeared to be a mischievous smile and replied, "I'll race you to the beach!"

The friendly wolf and healing girl sprinted off together in the direction of the ocean.

CHAPTER 6
TRUTH

Freedom was ten paces ahead of Sophia, his tail bobbing back and forth as he darted between the trees. Sophia smiled to herself while trying to catch him. She took pride in the fact she could outrun every kid in her class, and she was determined to run side-by-side with the wolf. When Sophia was getting close, Freedom jumped onto a large rock and used the hard surface to project himself forward. He flew gracefully through the air with all four legs fully extended like a ballerina. Sophia darted around the rock and leaped up as high as she could with her arms and legs stretched outward, mimicking her furry friend. Feeling free, she laughed with delight.

As they continued their playful run through the forest, Sophia noticed how strong her body felt. She was fully tuned into the movement of her leg muscles and her pumping arms as she sped between the giant trees. She and Freedom were running so fast that the details of her surroundings were lost on her; all she noticed was a green blur of foliage. Her focus was on her friend. Periodically she had to squint from a ray of sun breaking through the canopy of trees. It would blind her for a moment and then disappear. The only constant was the smell of clay dirt mixed with the moisture in the air.

She didn't know if her canine competitor was slowing down or if she was speeding up, but suddenly Sophia was running by the wolf's side. Every few paces they'd exhale aloud at the same time, their breathing in sync. She looked down at Freedom and he returned her glance with that playful twinkle in his eyes. Sophia felt a burst of joy in her heart. She looked ahead and saw an opening in the trees where the sun-filled beach met the shaded forest border. Together they arrived at the beach.

As the two friends walked upon the sand, Sophia realized they had circled back to the birthday campsite where she first met her wolf friend. She thought about how Grandma Judy would have loved meeting Freedom and Grace. It occurred to her that maybe Grandma Judy had sent them to her. That thought warmed Sophia's heart and brought a smile to her face.

"Look at the top of that large evergreen tree to your right," Freedom said as he pointed his snout in the direction of the towering tree at the cusp of the beach.

Sophia saw a huge bald eagle resting on a branch at the crest of the tree. She had seen eagles fly over the water near her home before. She recalled a time when she and Tara were walking across the low bridge over to a nearby island and encountered one. An eagle was riding the wind, floating just 10 feet overhead. The commanding bird had squawked at the girls while hovering above them, allowing time to inspect the bird's underside and outstretched wings. When the eagle finally flew away, they looked at each other and joyfully laughed over the gift they had received from the bird that flies highest in the sky.

The eagle looked down at Sophia and Freedom, and then suddenly took flight. He soared in the mountain's direction, flying higher and higher until he caught a breeze and then glided across the sky. Sophia saw there was no effort in the eagle's actions, no resistance. He allowed the natural forces in the sky to carry him. The thought occurred to her that if the eagle had everything within and around him to soar, maybe she did, too. She had just discovered she had animal friends looking out for her for her entire life. Maybe everything she needed to fly above her family situation and feel free was within and around her as well.

Suddenly the eagle lowered its head and began to speed swiftly in their direction. Sophia felt excited. As the bird approached, he slowed down, lifted his wings, and gently landed on Freedom's back. The eagle quickly turned his head from side to side, then looked directly at Sophia. Just as with Freedom and Grace, Sophia could hear the bird speaking to her from within herself.

"Hello, Sophia. My name is Truth. We've met before, you and me. Do you remember?"

Sophia couldn't believe it! This was the bald eagle from the bridge, and he remembered her.

"Yes! Of course! How could I forget?"

Sophia knelt next to her wolf guide so she could be at eye level with Truth.

"I've seen how difficult things have been for you, Sophia. The pain and loneliness you have experienced does not define the truth of who you are. You are as close to the heavens as I am, for you carry the divine spirit within you.

"You have received sound guidance from Freedom and Grace on your travels today. There is one more journey left, but this one you must do alone. As always, Freedom, Grace and I will be watching over you."

Sophia felt fear in her body.

"Why do I have to do this alone?"

The eagle looked into Sophia's eyes. Suddenly she had an image of herself soaring through the skies side-by-side with the powerful bird, looking directly into its left eye. She noticed the golden color of its iris and a strength that penetrated from its pupil. Sophia blinked and was back in her body on the beach.

"This is a journey within yourself, Sophia. It is one intended for all of us, although not everyone chooses to travel it. I've seen your courage and I know you are ready. Do you trust me that you will be safe?"

Sophia nodded her head up and down. She did trust this bird, just as much as she had trusted Grandma Judy and the same way she trusted Freedom and Grace.

"Very good. Sit down in a comfortable position, close your eyes and follow my instructions."

Sophia sat on the beach and closed her eyes. Truth told her to take a deep breath in.

"Notice with the inhale how your chest rises as your lungs fill with air. Hold your breath for a few moments and then slowly release it. Feel the air leave your body on your exhale and imagine it clearing away all the worries and hurt you have. Repeat these deep, cleansing breaths two more times."

Truth waited for Sophia's third breath before saying, "Now relax, keeping your eyes closed, breathing naturally."

Sophia followed Truth's instructions, noticing her body's restful state.

The bald eagle then said, "In your imagination, get up from where you are sitting on the beach and walk back down the path from which you and Freedom came."

The bird paused, allowing Sophia to create the picture in her mind.

"Now imagine the path leads you to a cave with a round wooden door at the entrance. Open the door and step inside. Notice how dark it is inside the cave except for the faint glow of an emerald light off in the distance."

Truth paused to allow Sophia time to create the image in her mind.

"Follow the path inside the cave; continue heading toward that light."

Sophia could see the cave door, the path and the glowing light inside her mind's eye. She envisioned herself walking down a circular path toward the center of the earth. Although the path was dark except for the distant light, Sophia no longer felt fear. She felt safe and was eager to see where the light was coming from.

In her mind, she followed the circular path around several times and then the path opened to an expansive cavern. She walked into the spacious cavern. There were rocks of all sizes scattered about, each with the same deep-green glassy exterior. Sophia felt compelled to touch one. She bent down and picked up a small rock that fit into the palm of her hand. She rubbed her thumb across its bumpy surface. She looked around and realized all the rocks had the same surface except for a large one that emerged out from the earth. It was several yards away.

Sophia walked over to examine the large rock. It was the same type as the others but had been split in half; one half lay on the ground while the other half stood erect. Sophia walked around the rock structure to inspect all sides of it. She gasped when she saw its backside; she stood frozen. The green rock had a smooth mirrored surface that reflected a bright light. She realized this was the source of the glowing light that lit her path. As she looked at the rock she began to weep. This time her tears were not from grief; they were tears of awe and joy.

The girl fell to her knees, humbled from the weight of her insight. Sophia recognized that the light was not coming from the rock. She realized the rock was a giant split moldavite, its shiny surface reflecting a light that was projecting out from Sophia's chest. In that moment Sophia understood that the love and strength her grandmother had given her was always within herself. The source was not outside her in a small piece of meteoric rock channeling her grandmother's love. The source of light was the love from which she was created -- and it still existed within her.

Sophia suddenly recalled Grandma Judy's words on her tenth birthday, "I love you and the source that created all that is loves you. Always remember there is nothing you can do or experience that can alter the spark within you. You are love and you are surrounded by love always. You are never, ever alone." Sophia now knew what her grandmother meant, and she recognized her own spark.

Sophia looked at her reflection again in the giant piece of moldavite and smiled broadly. She stood tall and took a snapshot with her mind. She wanted to be able to recall this image of herself with love's light shining out from her center. She wanted to capture the warmth she felt within when she acknowledged this truth. She took a deep breath in the same way the eagle had instructed her to when he prepared her for her solo journey. On the exhale, she gave thanks for the incredible lessons she received from her animal friends.

Sophia slowly opened her eyes. She found herself lying on the wet ground of Hope Island. She was surrounded by ferns, her life vest under her head, and a long black eagle's feather on the ground in front of her.

CHAPTER 7
HOPE

Sophia felt disoriented at first. She sat up, stretched her arms into the air, and rubbed her eyes. She wasn't sure if she was really seeing an eagle feather in front of her or if it was a remnant of a dream. She reached out and picked up the feather.

"The journey was real!" Sophia exclaimed.

She inspected the feather closely as she flashed back to her encounters with Freedom, Grace, and Truth. They had shown her who she really was inside and how to deal with her troubles. She realized that while her grandmother's gemstone was still broken, she now had Truth's feather to remind her of what she had learned on her journey. Sophia unzipped her backpack and gently put the feather inside to keep it safe for the paddle back to the mainland. She zipped up the bag, put it on her back, and got up.

With a newborn sense of confidence, Sophia grabbed her life jacket and began the hike back to the beach. She noticed she was smiling; she enjoyed the knowledge that she was never alone. When she reached her grandma's kayak, she took off her backpack and tucked it inside. She then pulled the kayak into the water and climbed in.

As Sophia started to paddle, she was struck by how different she felt from her frantic paddle out to Hope Island just a short time ago. Now, heading back to the mainland, she felt strong. She thought about the way Truth revealed the spark of love within her. It occurred to her that since everyone was created from that same love, it meant her dad and mom have that spark within them, too. Something may be covering it up, preventing their light from shining through, but it *must* be there. She reflected on the technique Grace gave her to still her mind and body, connecting her with her wise one within and tapping into her own power. She recalled Freedom's message to allow her feelings to flow and to use her voice to tell a safe adult what is happening in her life.

When Sophia arrived on shore she climbed out of the kayak and turned to face her island refuge. She pulled the eagle's feather out from her backpack and held it in her hands.

As she looked across the ocean inlet to the tree-filled land mass, she shouted, "I am love and I am connected to all that is!"

In that moment she made a pact with herself. Starting tomorrow she was going to spend the first five minutes of each day stilling her mind and body; whenever she felt upset, she was going to do the "Salute to the Sun" stretches or crank her favorite music up loud and dance; and she was going to tell Miss Shekinah about her home life.

For the first time in her life, Sophia felt what the Island's name promised.

WORKBOOK

WORKBOOK

Grandma Judy, Freedom, Grace and Truth gave Sophia several tools for her to use on her healing journey. You can use them as well. There is no wrong way to apply them. Pick and choose the practices and activities on the following pages that resonate best with you and give them your own personal touch.

JOURNALING/ DISCUSSION QUESTIONS

Journaling can be a good way to come to understand how you feel about a situation and it can be a powerful emotional release. When you plan to journal, first take a few deep breaths to relax yourself to connect with your "wise one within."

Below are several questions related to the *Hope Island* story that can be answered through journaling or by discussing your answers with a trusted person or group. Reflect on a question and then write or share your response. Take your time with each question; they are not intended to be answered in one writing session or discussion.

Safe Places

- Hope Island is Sophia's physical safe place. She finds undisturbed quiet time there, and she feels safe because the island reminds her of her Grandma Judy's love. Also, being surrounded by nature helps Sophia to relax. Do you have an indoor or an outdoor "Hope Island" you like to retreat to in order to calm down and feel safe?
  - If so, describe your safe place. What do you see, feel, hear and smell?
  - If not, read the "Creating a Place of Safety" section of this book.

Safe Relationships

- Why was Grandma Judy so important to Sophia?
- Do you have someone like Grandma Judy in your life?
  - If so, who is that and what makes that person special to you?
  - If not, imagine having someone like Grandma Judy in your life and describe what that person says and does when they are with you.
- Tara was Sophia's "virtual safe place." She allowed Sophia to talk about her troubles without judging her, laughing at her, or telling anyone her secrets. Tara was compassionate and understanding. Do you have a friend like Tara you can trust?
  - If so, describe your friend and what helps you know they are safe.

JOURNALING/DISCUSSION QUESTIONS

- o If not, imagine having a friend like Tara in your life that you can share anything with and feel safe. Describe what that person says and does when they are with you and why you know they are safe.
    - NOTE: To test if someone can be a safe friend like Tara, start by sharing something small that won't hurt you if that person tells someone else. Make it clear you want it to remain private between the two of you. If they honor your request and they don't talk behind your back, share something more to test again if this friend is safe. Continue to slowly disclose more and more as your friend demonstrates trustworthiness. If they consistently honor your friendship, you are on your way to having a safe, trusted friend in your life.
- Why did Sophia hesitate to tell an adult outside of her family what was going on in her home?
- Do you have a trusted adult in your life like Miss Shekinah you can talk to? What secrets would you share with that person?

Symbols

- What meaning did Grandma Judy's moldavite necklace have for Sophia?
    - o What helps you to feel connected to other people?
    - o What helps you to feel connected to nature?

- What helps you to feel connected to your True Self?
- What does the word "freedom" mean to you?
  - For you, what animal, person, object, or place symbolizes freedom?
- Freedom pointed out to Sophia that it was courageous of her to stand up to her dad. The wolf also acknowledged it can be scary to tell someone outside of her family about the family secrets.
  - For you, what animal, person, object, or place symbolizes courage?
- What does the word "grace" mean to you?
  - For you, what animal, person, object, or place symbolizes grace?
- What does the word "truth" mean to you?
  - For you, what animal, person, object, or place represents your truth or True Self?
- What did the eagle feather symbolize for Sophia?
- If you could choose any animal or being to watch over you and to be your guide, who or what would that be and why?

Lessons from the Animals

- What did Sophia learn from Freedom, her wolf guide?
- What feelings had Sophia been keeping inside? When was the last time you felt that way? What happened?
- Sophia is going to dance to her favorite music and do the "Salute to the Sun" stretches when

JOURNALING/DISCUSSION QUESTIONS

she feels upset. What physical activities would be fun ways for you to move and to release negative energy from your body when you feel upset?
- What did Grace, Sophia's deer friend, teach her to do?
- What was the message from Sophia's "wise one within"?
- What explanation did Truth, the bald eagle, give Sophia for having to take the final journey on her own?

CREATING A PLACE OF SAFETY

Physical Safe Place

Sophia used Hope Island as her physical safe place – a place where she reconnected with feelings of love and safety. You can create a safe place for yourself as well. When creating a safe place, it can be as simple as climbing a favorite tree in your yard if you have one, or as extravagant as decorating a corner of your bedroom. Below are several suggestions for making a safe place.

- **Location:** Choose a location in which you already feel comfortable and are free to retreat to when you are feeling upset. It can be a place in your home or a place outside.
- **Symbols:** Place an item in your safe place that will remind you of the eternal spark of love

that exists within you. For Sophia, the moldavite necklace initially was this token. At the end of the story, the eagle feather she found on the ground on Hope Island became that token. Consider what your token can be to symbolize this truth for you. The "Journaling/Discussion Questions – Lessons from the Animals" section above had questions regarding symbols for freedom, grace, truth and courage. If you answered those questions, maybe one or more of the symbols you came up with are right for your safe place.

- **Soothing Items:** Place items in your safe place that help you to soothe yourself. The more senses you engage, the better. Items that smell nice, like flowers, lavender spray, perfume, or scented candles work well. A nice scented hand lotion works great, too, because it engages your sense of touch when you rub the lotion on your skin, plus it engages your sense of smell with its scent. Another safe-place item that stimulates the sense of touch is a stuffed animal or doll. When we give a hug, we get a hug, even when it's a stuffed toy. If you have a stuffed toy you loved on when you were younger, maybe it can have a new home in your safe place. For visual stimulation, you could include a picture of a scene that you love, or a picture of one of your symbols as described in the "Symbols" paragraph above. For example, a picture in your safe place of a beautiful stream could be a reminder of the freedom you experience when allowing your feelings to flow.

- **Calming and Centering Activities:** One of the most important aspects of having a safe place is what you do there to feel your feelings, release them, and calm yourself. Read the "Calming and Centering Activities" section of this workbook and choose one or more to practice in your safe place.

Having a safe place to go to when you're upset or need a break isn't just for the home. The Safe Place comes from Dr. Becky Bailey's Conscious Discipline®, an approach to healing homes and schools, and it is being used all over the world!

Virtual Safe Place

When Sophia met the animal friends in her dream, she learned how to create another type of safe place – one within herself. She learned ways to breathe deeply and to use her imagination to create a sense of peace and well-being inside. By practicing the calming and centering activities in the next section, you can create a safe place within yourself that you can visit anytime, anywhere. Start by imagining the token or symbol you have chosen to remind you of the eternal spark of love that exists within you, and then begin applying one of the activities.

CALMING AND CENTERING ACTIVITIES

Grandma Judy's Love and Appreciation Breath

This breathing exercise can be done anytime. It can help you to calm down when you are feeling upset. It can also be done as a daily practice for several minutes.

Take a deep breath, imagining you are inhaling love through your heart. Hold in your mind the image of a person, place, or thing you appreciate. On the exhale, imagine you are sending appreciation out through your heart to that person, place, or thing. Next, imagine that appreciation expanding out to your community, across your country, and across the planet. Continue to imagine you are breathing love in and appreciation out through your heart. Open your eyes when you feel ready.

Salute to the Sun

> *I raise my hands to the radiant sun.*
> *I welcome its light shining on us as one.*
> *I wave to the eagle flying high in the sky.*
> *I shrug off my worries to let them flow by.*
> *I touch the land surrounded by sea.*
> *I see love's light in you and me.*

This stretch can be done with a partner, in front of a mirror, or by yourself while imagining someone or something you appreciate in front of you.

1. Take a slow, deep breath in through your nostrils and then slowly let the air out through your mouth. On each exhale push the air out making a long "haa" sound the way you would if you were trying to fog up a window or mirror. Try to make the exhale last twice as long as the inhale. Repeat these deep breaths three times.
2. Next, breathe normally. Notice your chest moving gently up and down as your body relaxes.
3. Say, "I raise my hands to the radiant sun," as you stretch your arms up in the air. If you are not outside or can't see the sun, imagine the golden globe in the sky.
4. Say, "I welcome its light shining on us as one," as you open your arms wide in a V-shape.
5. Say, "I wave to the eagle flying high in the sky," as you sway your arms back and forth a few times.
6. Bring your arms to your sides.
7. Say, "I shrug off my worries to let them flow by," as you roll your shoulders a few times.

8. Say, "I touch the land surrounded by sea," while reaching toward the ground or floor. Keep your legs as straight as you can with your knees slightly bent. It's okay if you can't touch the ground. It's the relaxed stretch that you want.
9. Lastly, make a heart shape with your fingers as you say, "I see love's light in you and me." If you are doing this with a partner, look your partner in the eyes and extend your finger heart out toward them. If you are doing this in a mirror, look yourself in the eyes and extend the heart toward your reflection.

Grace's Stillness Meditation

We live in a busy world with lots of information and stimulation all around us. It seems our minds are always active. Sometimes there is so much noise in our heads that it's hard to know how we feel inside. Learning to still your mind and body can help you to stay centered and to connect with your feelings. Follow Grace's instructions below to practice stilling your mind and body. Making a daily practice of this, even for just a few minutes, can make a big difference in your general well-being.

1. Take three slow, deep cleansing breaths. On each inhale say to yourself, "Peace to my mind." On each exhale say, "Still my thoughts and body."
2. After you finish your third breath, relax, breathing naturally. Focus on your breathing, noticing each inhale and exhale. When your thoughts wander from noticing your breath, simply repeat

"Peace to my mind. Still my thoughts and body," and continue to focus on your breath.

3. Continue this relaxed breathing for a few minutes. Over time, try to extend the duration.

Truth's Guided Journey

Truth guided Sophia on an imaginary journey that helped her to discover her connection to her True Self: love. You can do the same thing for yourself. Use a recording device, such as a voice recording app on a cell phone, to record yourself reading the script in italics below. With a warm, relaxed voice, read it very slowly, pausing after each sentence to allow yourself time to imagine the scene. Once you have the recording, find a place where you can sit quietly, such as your safe place. Close your eyes, listen to the recording, and follow the instructions.

Another option is to make up your own guided journey to your True Self that you record and listen to. Use your imagination and have fun with it!

SCRIPT:

Close your eyes and take three deep, cleansing breaths. Notice when you inhale how your chest rises as your lungs fill with air and gently lowers on your exhale, releasing the air.

Now relax, keeping your eyes closed. Allow your body to breathe naturally.

Picture yourself standing in a forest of trees. There is green vegetation all around you and an earthy scent in the air. In front of you, there is a cave with a round wooden door. See yourself open the door and step inside. Visualize it being dark inside the cave except for a faint emerald glow from a light farther ahead in the cave. Follow a descending circular dirt path toward the light. Notice with each step of your descent that the light gets brighter.

After following the circular path a few times, see the cave open to an expansive cavern and walk in. Picture there are green glassy rocks of all sizes scattered about. Across the cavern, there is a large rock emerging out from the earth. Envision yourself walking slowly over to examine the rock.

Imagine the large rock is split in half, creating a smooth, mirrored surface. Stand in front of the rock mirror. There is a bright light projecting out from your chest and reflecting back at you from the shiny rock. Take a deep breath in and let it out slowly. Acknowledge this light is the eternal spark of love that exists within you. It is the unalterable source from which you came and forever lights your path.

Sit in silence for a few moments to absorb this truth.

Take a deep breath in, inhaling an appreciation for your constant connection to this Life Force; exhale with the thought, "This is my Truth."

Take one more deep cleansing breath.

When you are ready, open your eyes.

GRATITUDE PRACTICES

Gratitude Reflection

Feelings of appreciation have the power to positively shift how we feel inside. A Gratitude Reflection connects you with these feelings. It is as simple as thinking about the people, places, situations, or things in your life you appreciate. State them either in your mind or aloud by saying something like, "I am thankful for ...," or, "I appreciate ...," or, "I give thanks for ...," and fill in the blank with whatever it is you are appreciating in that moment. You can close with an affirming statement such as, "My heart is filled with gratitude." In the *Hope Island* story, when Grandma Judy did a Gratitude Reflection during Sophia's tenth birthday camp-side dinner, she closed with, "We open our hearts and receive this love with gratitude."

You can create a gratitude reflection of your own in any moment for anything. There is no wrong way to do it. The more you practice these, the more you transform your inner state to a positive one.

Gratitude Journal

Another good way to connect with feelings of gratitude is to reflect each day on at least three things for which you are thankful and write them down in a Gratitude Journal. A Gratitude Journal is basically a record of your daily Gratitude Reflections that you either list like a log or write about like a diary. Many people find this to be a good practice to do before they go to bed each night. You can make a Gratitude Journal by simply putting three-holed paper in a binder to use, or you can purchase a blank journal at a store or website that sells books.

Gratitude Jar

A fun way to practice gratitude is to use a clear, empty jar with a lid and small pieces of paper to create a Gratitude Jar. When you think of something or someone for which you're thankful, write it on a small piece of paper, fold it up, and stick it in the jar. If you want to make it colorful, cut up small pieces of wrapping paper and write your gratitude notes on the blank side. Your Gratitude Jar can be used in several ways.

- On the last day of each month, read all your gratitude notes to celebrate the abundance of goodness in your life.
- On days when you are feeling down, pull out one (or more) of your gratitude notes and read it to yourself. This can help you to remember

something positive. You can even go one step further and tape the gratitude note to a mirror or wall in your room to help remind you there is something in your life you appreciate.

- If it's possible, ask your family to create a Family Gratitude Jar to which everyone contributes. When you sit down together for a meal, pull out one of the gratitude notes and read it aloud. The note can remain anonymous, or the family members can have fun guessing who the author is. This can also be done with your chosen family – your friends!

POSITIVE AFFIRMATIONS

Feelings follow thoughts, and thoughts follow beliefs. The power in this is that you can choose to change your thoughts and beliefs, which will ultimately change how you feel inside. A daily practice of affirming positive truths about yourself can rewire how you think and feel.

Affirmation Statements

An affirmation is a statement that is declared to be true. The brain likes to have a goal. Using a positive affirmation gives it a good goal. Creating an affirmation that is positive about yourself will help your brain to spot evidence of what you are affirming. For example, "I am love," is a positive affirmation. If you say it often enough, you will likely come to see that it's true and believe it. Unfortunately, the same thing happens when you use negative affirmations, such as, "I'm so stupid!" When you have this negative thought, your brain searches and finds examples of when you've made a mistake, which we all have, reinforcing this negative belief about yourself.

To begin creating your positive affirmation, consider something good about yourself that you can affirm each day. You can use a starter phrase, such as, "I am," or, "I can," and then state the goodness you are affirming. You can have one affirmation you are working with or several affirming statements. For example, at the end of the *Hope Island* story, Sophia affirmed, "I am love and I am connected to all that is!"

Print your affirmation(s) on a piece of paper to post somewhere you are likely to see every day, such as a bedroom wall or a bathroom mirror. If you've created a physical safe place for yourself, that is also a good place to post your affirmation(s).

If you find yourself struggling to come up with affirmations, below are some examples. A quick internet search on "affirmations for teens" will yield hundreds to choose from.

Sample Affirmations		
I am love.	I am loved.	I am loving.
I am safe.	I am worthy.	I am bright.
I am helpful.	I am trustworthy.	I am getting better every day.
I feel calm.	I trust in my abilities.	I make good decisions.
I can do it.	I have courage.	I learn from my mistakes.
I can do whatever I focus my mind on.	I am gentle with myself and others.	My intuition is a guide showing me the right direction.

Another way to come up with positive affirmations is to make a list of all the negative statements you commonly say to yourself and flip them into the opposite. The chart below provides a few examples of flipping a negative statement into a positive affirmation.

Affirmation Flip	
Negative Statement	Positive Affirmation
I am stupid.	I am bright.
I can't do anything right.	I can do it.
I am a wreck.	I feel calm.
I am worthless.	I am worthy.

If you find you are resisting the positive affirmation because it doesn't feel true yet, begin your affirmation with, "I am willing to believe that …," or, "I am open to the possibility that …" These phrases can create a bridge between where you are today and ultimately believing your affirmation. Using Sophia's example, if her affirmation didn't feel comfortable yet, she could write, "I am willing to believe that I am love," or, "I am open to the possibility that I am connected to all that is." If you use a bridge affirmation, try the direct affirmation again after a few weeks to see if it feels more comfortable. If not, continue with your bridge affirmation.

Affirmation Poster

An affirmation poster is simply a poster with your affirmation(s) that you decorate in a colorful way. You can print inspiring pictures from the internet or cut pictures out of magazines to put on your poster. You can also paint or draw on your poster, put stickers on it, any combination of these, and more. Like the affirmation statement, your affirmation poster can go in your safe place or anywhere else easily visible to you.

For example, if Sophia were to create an affirmation poster after returning from her Hope Island journey, she might print on her poster, "I am love and I am connected to all that is!" Or, she might print a bridge affirmation such as, "I am open to the possibility that I am love and connected to all that is." She might add, "I am safe. I allow my feelings to flow. I share my feelings with trusted friends." She would possibly download pictures from the internet of a wolf, a deer, and a bald eagle, and paste them to her poster. She could even stick her True Self token – the eagle feather – to her affirmation poster.

Your affirmation poster is for you. Go ahead and express your unique self!

HELP

In the *Hope Island* story, Sophia appreciated being able to talk to her grandmother and later to Tara about her troubles. She also learned from her animal friends that adult help was available outside her home, and so she planned to speak with her teacher, Miss Shekinah, about her home life.

In addition to teachers and school counselors, there are many organizations and groups available to support someone dealing with difficult life situations. Below are just a few.

Referrals

- Rape, Abuse & Incest National Network (RAINN) is the nation's largest anti-sexual violence organization. RAINN created and operates the National Sexual Assault Telephone Hotline that connects callers with a trained

staff member from a sexual assault service provider in their area.
- Hotline is 1-800-656-HOPE (4673) and website is https://rainn.org and https://rainn.org/es for Spanish
• National Suicide Prevention Lifeline has trained crisis workers available to talk 24 hours a day, 7 days a week.
- Helpline is 1-800-273-8255 and website is https://suicidepreventionlifeline.org
• To Write Love on Her Arms (TWLOHA) is a non-profit organization dedicated to presenting hope and finding help for people struggling with depression, self-injury, addiction, and suicide. TWLOHA exists to encourage, inform, inspire, and to invest directly into treatment and recovery.
- Website is https://twloha.com
• Substance Abuse and Mental Health Services Administration (SAMHSA) Treatment Referral.
- Helpline is 1-800-662-HELP and website https://findtreatment.samhsa.gov

12 Step Recovery Programs

• Al-Anon is a mutual support program for people whose lives have been affected by someone else's drinking.
- Website is https://al-anon.org
• Alateen, a part of the Al-Anon Family Groups, is a fellowship of young people (mostly teenagers) whose lives have been affected by someone

else's drinking whether they are in your life drinking or not. The teens come together to share experiences to find effective ways to cope with problems. Alateen meetings can be found on the Al-Anon website.

- Adult Children of Alcoholics® (ACA)/Dysfunctional Families is a twelve-step/twelve tradition program of men and women who grew up in alcoholic or otherwise dysfunctional homes. They meet to share their experience of growing up in an environment where abuse, neglect and trauma infected them, and to share their recovery from its effects.
  - Website is https://adultchildren.org

www.ingramcontent.com/pod-product-compliance
Lightning Source LLC
Chambersburg PA
CBHW071220070526
44584CB00019B/3095